FIVE
backstage pass
A Rockin' Keepsake Scrapbook

By Michael-Anne Johns

SCHOLASTIC INC.

New York   Toronto   London   Auckland   Sydney   Mexico City   New Delhi   Hong Kong

W9-CAG-006

Photography Credits:
Front Cover: Anthony Cutajar; Back Cover: Anthony Cutajar/London Features; 1: Bernhard Kuhmstedt/Retna; 3: David Fisher/London Features; 4: Bernhard Kuhmstedt/Retna; 5, top: Jon Super/Retna; 5, bottom: James McCauley/Retna; 6, top: James McCauley/Retna; 6, bottom: Fred Duval/Famous; 7, top: Dennis Van Tine/London Features; 7, bottom: Dennis Nadalin; 8: Anthony Cutajar; 9, top: Bernhard Kuhmstedt/Retna; 9, bottom: Retna; 10: Anthony Cutajar; 11: Jadranka Krsteska/Famous; 12: Bernhard Kuhmstedt/Retna; 13, top: Anthony Cutajar; 13, bottom: Simon Meaker/Retna; 14: Scott Robinson/Retna; 15: Dennis Nadalin; 16: Bernhard Kuhmstedt/Retna; 17, top: James McCauley/Retna; 17, bottom: Anthony Cutajar; 18: Anthony Cutajar; 19, top: Colin Bell/Retna; 19, bottom: Jadranka Krsteska/Famous; 20: Bernhard Kuhmstedt/Retna; 21, top: Anthony Cutajar/London Features; 21, bottom: Dennis Nadalin; 22: Sean Colon/Retna; 23, top: Colin Bell/Retna; 23, bottom: Anthony Cutajar; 24-25: Anthony Cutajar; 26: Anthony Cutajar; 27, top: Bernhard Kuhmstedt/Retna; 27, bottom: James McCauley/Retna; 28: Bernhard Kuhmstedt/Retna; 29, top: Dennis Nadalin; 29, bottom: Jason Brown/Retna; 30, top left: Hugh Thompson/Retna; 30, bottom left: Dave Hogan/Retna; 30, top right: James McCauley/Retna; 30, bottom right: All Action; 31, top: Barry J. Holmes/Retna; 31, middle: Colin Mason/London Features; 31, bottom: Dennis Nadalin; 32, top left: Jadranka Krsteska/Famous; 32, bottom left: Simon Meaker/Retna; 32, top right: Retna; 32, bottom right: James McCauley/Retna; 33, top left: Simon Meaker/Retna; 33, bottom left: Eddie Malluk; 33, top right: Dennis Nadalin; 33, bottom right: N. Zuffante/Star File Photo; 34: Barry J. Holmes/Retna; 35: Anthony Cutajar; 36, top: Anthony Cutajar/London Features; 36, bottom: Retna; 37, top: Fred Duval/Famous; 37, bottom: Colin Mason/London Features; 38, top: Retna; 38, middle: Retna; 38, bottom: Anthony Cutajar; 39: Bernhard Kuhmstedt/Retna; 40, top: Peter Atchison/Famous; 40, bottom: Anthony Cutajar; 41: Anthony Cutajar; 42: Bernhard Kuhmstedt/Retna; 43: Fred Duval/Famous; 44, top: Fred Duval/Famous; 44, bottom: James McCauley/Retna; 45, top: Fred Duval/Famous; 45, bottom: Dennis Nadalin; 46: Colin Bell/Retna; 47: Anthony Cutajar; 48: Bernhard Kuhmstedt/Retna.

With love, to my niece Kimberly

If you purchased this book without a cover, you should be aware that this book is stolen property. It was reported as "unsold and destroyed" to the publisher, and neither the author nor the publisher has received any payment for this "stripped book."

No part of this work may be reproduced, stored in a retrieval system, or transmitted in any form or by any means, electronic, mechanical, photocopying, recording, or otherwise, without written permission of the publisher. For information regarding permission, write to Scholastic Inc., Attention: Permissions Department, 555 Broadway, New York, NY 10012.

ISBN 0-439-08797-X

Cover design by Jennifer Presant
Interior design by Peter Koblish

Copyright © 1999 Scholastic Inc. All rights reserved. Published by Scholastic Inc. SCHOLASTIC and associated logos are trademarks and/or registered trademarks of Scholastic Inc.

12 11 10 9 8 7 6 5 4 3   9/9 0 1 2 3 4/0

Printed in the U.S.A.
First Scholastic printing, August 1999

Contents

Join the Party of FIVE!

FIVE...**5**...**five**...**5ive**...no matter how you add it up or spell it out, FIVE is the band for the new millennium!

British boys Rich Neville, Scott Robinson, Abs Breen, Sean Conlon, and J Brown are FIVE. Since they first broke out in England with the jump-to-your-feet single, "Slam Dunk (Da Funk)," they've been the toast of teens in Europe. FIVE fever spread across the Atlantic when they debuted their U.S. single, "When the Lights Go Out." That was just a tasty tease of things to come.

But let's not get ahead of ourselves — rewind to the beginning of their once-upon-a-time story.

J

Rich

Scott

Abs

Sean

Talent Search

In 1996, father-and-son music management team Bob and Chris Herbert made headlines as the brainiacs who came up with the idea for the Spice Girls. Bob and Chris figured if "girl power" caught on, a "*boy bonanza*" was a snap!

So, just as they'd done for the Spice Girls, the Herberts put out the call — this time they advertised for young *male* singers and dancers in the music industry magazine *The Stage*. Auditions were held all over England. Over 3,000 would-be and wannabe lads turned out, but when it came to the final pick, it was Rich, Scott, Abs, Sean, and J all the way. At the time, they ranged in age from sixteen (Sean) to twenty-one (J).

"With everything we learned with the Spice Girls, we wanted to bring together a new boy act," Chris Herbert explained when they finally introduced FIVE to the press. "But not the usual crop of boy bands — we wanted a band with attitude and edge. As soon as we saw these five guys, we knew they had it both musically and character-wise."

From day one, it was obvious that the FIVE mix was something special. Besides great singing voices, they all brought much more to the party. Rich had experience as an actor and as the lead singer in several bands; Scott had taken acting classes; Abs had also studied theater and was a rapper and DJ; Sean had been singing and writing songs (he'd won the prestigious Yamaha Young Composer competition when he was just thirteen); J had built a studio in his bedroom and rapped with several hot crews.

Check out FIVE — *live*.

Roommates and "Noise Pollution"?

Just days after the final audition, Bob and Chris
moved all five boys into a house in the Surrey section
right outside of London. "One minute I was taking my A-
levels [British standard tests], the next I was sharing a
house with four guys I'd never met before," laughs Rich.
"But we really got to know each other." Scott adds: "We
hit it off straight away. We all just gelled together."

Every day the boys worked nonstop on their
singing and dancing. From the beginning, their individual voices and styles clicked; there was no attempt
to "create" a group look or attitude for them. There
wasn't going to be a FIVE uniform on- or offstage. Each member had a different streetwise edge to his personality, which gave FIVE a certain "bad-boy" flavor. You
never knew *what* was going to happen when Rich, Scott, Abs, Sean, and J got together.

Scott and Abs do some
preconcert bonding.

What eventually took shape, quite naturally, was a chaotic blend of rap, alternative, pop, and even classical music echoing day and night from the FIVE house. An electric energy vibrated as they perfected their act.

"It was a complete madhouse," Scott recalls of the raucous residence. "We ended up getting chucked by the housing council. A bit of noise pollution, you know."

The lads from FIVE are all about having fun with their fans.

Noise *pollution*? That's not what British teens concluded when FIVE released their first single, "Slam Dunk (Da Funk)." Indeed, *Smash Hits* magazine named FIVE "Best New Band" at their 1997 awards show. FIVE followed "Slam Dunk" with "When the Lights Go Out," which entered the UK charts at #4 and quickly rose to the #1 spot.

Since then FIVE has been dominating the pop charts in Europe, Asia, Australia, and Canada. In 1998, the babe-alicious boys invaded the shores of the U.S. "When the Lights Go Out" jumped on the pop charts and remained lodged firmly in the Top 10 for the next 20 weeks. And so FIVE-mania began.

See where it's going!

Tidbit #1
It's All in a Name

When British mags first wrote about FIVE, they used the *number* 5; then they changed it to 5IVE. Finally, word had it the record company wanted it spelled out FIVE. When asked about this "controversy," Abs told *Smash Hits*: "I haven't got a clue what that's about. It's just a creative thing, I think. One of us had probably written it with a number and we'd liked it. It just sort of carried on from there. How should fans write it? Any way you want to, mate. You do what you want!"

RICH
The Cute One

The British teen mags dubbed Rich Neville "Rich Five." But when U.S. fans first saw FIVE on MTV, they dubbed him "the cute one." Of course, that's not to say Scott, Abs, Sean, and J aren't cute — but Rich, he's in a league of his own.

Unsurprisingly, Rich first started his showbiz career as an actor. "I did a lot of acting at school," he revealed in a *Smash Hits* interview. "I played Romeo in *Romeo and Juliet,* Danny in *Grease,* all sorts. . . ."

At that point Rich was quickly interrupted by the *Smash Hits* reporter, and asked to "speaketh some Shakespearean lines." Always eager to please, Rich began in a hushed voice, "But soft, what light through yonder window breaks? It is the east and Juliet is the sun. . . . 'Tis my lady, oh, 'tis my love."

Big sigh! Needless to say, Rich won over a few more fans that day. Actually, acting is a big part of Rich's life, and he hopes to return to the stage one day. "I wouldn't leave FIVE, not at the moment," he assured the reporter. "Besides, I think to be a good actor you've got to have a lot of life experience."

For now Rich is definitely getting a lot of life experience with FIVE, but he knows that there will be a day when he and his mates will want to move on. At that point, Rich feels he'll have a lot of options. "I'd like to carry on singing, definitely, and I'd like to act," he told *Teen*. "I know it sounds cliché, but performing is a part of me."

Rich gets goofy on the set of **FIVE**'s *Now & Forever* video.

In his own words:
• What FIVE means to Rich •

F is for funkiness!

I is for individual, because that's what the band is!

V is for Venus, because we're out of this world!

E is for energy — we're full of it!

Rich Stats

Full Name: Richard Neville
Nicknames: Rich, Ritchie, Posh
B-day: August 23, 1979
Birthplace: Solihul, Birmingham, England
Astro Sign: Virgo
Height: 5'9"
Hair/Eyes: Brown/Blue
Shoe Size: Nine
Parents: Peter and Kim (they divorced when he was two years old)
Siblings: Older sister, Tracey, and older brother, Dave
Early Jobs: Sold hamburgers in a food van; worked in his mother's pub, the Crab Mill in Bromsgrove

Tender Tidbits

Childhood Hero: Pearl Jam's Eddie Vedder
Roommate in the FIVE House: J
Dream Girl: A mix of Michelle Pfeiffer and Cameron Diaz
Hobbies: Dating, listening to music, going to clubs
Major Dislike: Conceited people
Boxers or Briefs: Calvin Klein boxers
First Record Bought: Pet Shop Boys' *Rent*
Worst Fear: Spiders
Food Yucks: Sprouts, currants, quiche
Scariest Moment: "I was onstage and I touched some [fans] and they grabbed my finger. I nearly lost my ring that day."
Sleep Secrets: He snores.
Secret Blush: When Rich was five, he thought he was Spiderman.
Self-Analysis: "Very soft, open, and emotional"
Worst Quality: "I'm impatient. If I want something, I want it *now*."

How does Rich make up after a breakup? "I would do whatever it takes — buy her flowers, special things — all the noble things," he says.

The first time Rich was in a primary-school Easter play: "The whole class dressed up as chickens," he recalls. "My mum's got a photograph of me dressed up!"

Worst Habit: Biting his nails

Best Purchase: Buying his dad a car — a Previa

If He Could Be an Animal: "I'd be a lion because it's the king of the jungle!"

Role in FIVE: "I'm the peacemaker. I'm quite a pacifist. I don't like people to be arguing. If it kicks off, say, that Scott wore J's trainers [sneakers] but didn't ask J, and J gets mad, I'll step in and work it out."

Little-Known Fact: Rich wears eyeglasses!

faves

FIVE Song: "'Slam Dunk (Da Funk)' because it was the song that we released first in Europe."

Book: *The Adventures of Adrian Mole*

Place: Cape Town, South Africa

Food: Chinese, Kentucky Fried Chicken

Drink: Tea with two sugars

Midnight Snack: Chocolate

School Subject: "Drama. I was the worst in math and I hated physics."

Vacation: "I went to Thailand with my family — it was really cool."

Holiday: Christmas

Christmas Dinner: "Turkey, spuds, and my mum does little sausages with bacon wrapped round 'em."

Theme Park: "Disneyland — my nephew Robert has always wanted to go, and I promised I would take him."

Sports: Rugby, football [soccer], and tennis.

Tidbit #2 Exclusive! Stop the Presses!
Rich told us everyone had been misspelling his nickname — it's Ritchie, with a 't'!

Aftershave: Hugo Boss, Joop!

Shampoo: Pantene

Actor: Sean Connery

Actress: Michelle Pfeiffer

Cartoon: *Dungeons and Dragons*

Superhero: Batman

Band: Pearl Jam

Pearl Jam Song: "'Jeremy' — this song got me through a few bad times. I went through this really weird phase a few years ago and [it] helped me through it."

Sports Shoes: Nike

Sleeping Position: Lying facedown, with one pillow under his head, and one to hug

Cuddle Toy: A teddy bear named Benson — a fan gave it to him for Christmas 1997.

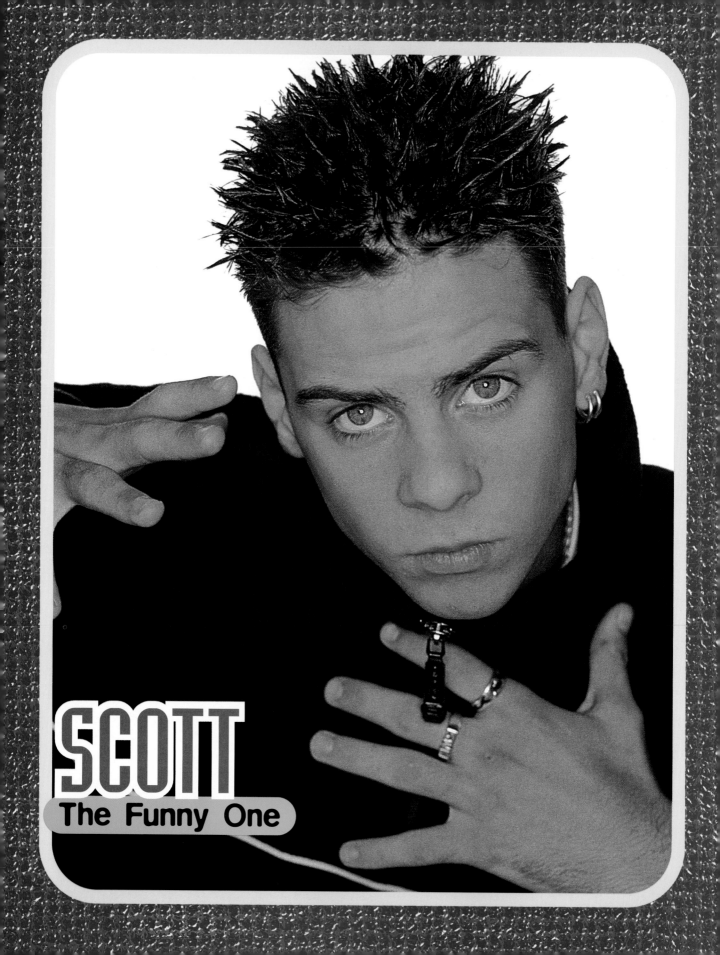

SCOTT
The Funny One

If you want to see Scott Robinson flip out, hide his hair gel! He knows he's a bit over-the-top about keeping his spiky hair porcupine-sharp, but he *can* joke about it. That's because Scott has a natural giggle streak and can see the humor in almost anything.

Scott's FIVE-mates all agree he's "the funny one." As if on cue, whenever they describe some of his hysterical antics, he'll be clowning around in the background.

But there's a method to Scott's silliness — he uses his humor to keep things nearly normal in the topsy-turvy world of pop stars. If J, Abs, Rich, or Sean is tired, irritable, or moody because they've been touring nonstop on no sleep, Scott will do something outrageous to lighten up the mood. If some tabloid reporter writes an article slagging him or FIVE, you can be sure Scott will come up with some lighthearted quote to squash the controversy.

Most of all, Scott tries not to take all the fame and fortune heaped on FIVE too seriously. He knows it's trouble when stars start believing the hype and forget who they really are and where they came from.

To that end, Scott has gone out of his way to stay tight with the friends he had before FIVE. "I don't class myself as a pop star," he told an Internet reporter. "I haven't dropped any of my mates. I know they're my real friends and they'll come up to me and give me a cuddle — even the lads!"

Every time he hears that fans think he's a babe, Scott actually gets embarrassed. Recently he told *Smash Hits*: "The first time I realized FIVE were considered sex symbols was when I was watching MTV with Abs and they had a phone vote on boys. Abs was number three and I was number five. It's quite a scary thing knowing girls are phoning in and voting for me. . . . It's weird that people rate me as being a good-looking lad. I don't get it because I'm just normal."

And humble!

In his own words:
• What FIVE means to Scott •

F is for funky
I is for imaginative
V is for vibing (you hear something new in every song!)
E is for educated

Scott Stats

Full Name: Scott James Tim Robinson

Nicknames: "I used to be called Spider because of my legs, and Curtains when I had long, floppy hair with a part in the middle."

B-day: November 22, 1979

Birthplace: Basildon in Essex, England

Astro Sign: Scorpio

Height: 5'11"

Hair/Eyes: Dark Brown/Blue

Parents: Mitch and Sue

Siblings: Older sisters, Nicola and Hayley

School: Sylvia Young Stage School

Pets: "I had a hamster named Lester, but it died."

Early Jobs: Actor — he appeared in theater, British TV series like *Eastenders*, and in commercials

Tender Tidbits

Childhood Hero: Knight Rider

Roommate in the FIVE House: Abs

Dream Girl: "I like a cute girl who likes to smile, someone who doesn't like to argue, and she's gotta be nice to me."

Best Friend: His hometown chum, Scott — "He looks like Nick Carter from the Backstreet Boys."

Hobby: Dancing

First Audition: For the play *Monty Moonbeam's Magnificent Mission* at the Towngate Theatre in Basildon — he went with his sister Nicola. They both got roles.

School Scoop: Scott had trouble until he found out he was dyslexic and learned how to study.

Scott plays down the fact that he's a cutey. He kids: "When I wake up in the morning, I look in the mirror and think, 'Oh, God, go back to sleep!'"

"I'm not vain," insists Scott. "I just try to make the most of what I've got. I look after myself, but that's not being vain. I think everyone should make the best of themselves."

Major Dislike: "Arguing — I don't see the point."

Boxers or Briefs: Calvin Klein boxers

Most Embarrassing Moment: "Anytime my hair isn't up to scratch — like the time I had a curly perm when I was in *Peter Pan*."

Worst Habits: Bites his nails and oversleeps

Secret Turn-on: "I love hugs. Hugs are just the best thing."

Special Turn-off: Creamy salad dressing — "touching it makes me sick!"

Least Fave Smell: Coconut — "It makes me want to heave!"

Photo Phobia: "I'll kick off [complain] if my mum gets a camera out [on holidays] because I have to face cameras every day of the week!"

Self-Analysis: "People say I make them laugh. I talk quite a lot, too."

Best Quality: "I think I'm quite a good person to talk to — you can talk to me about anything."

Worst Body Part: "My legs because they're too hairy."

Can't Live Without: "My hair wax!"

Scott's Hero: "My dad. He's a really cool dude. He's about forty-five, but he looks a lot younger." (*TV Hits*)

Worst Breakup: His first love broke up with him over the phone when he joined FIVE and the group went to Sweden to record their first album.

Tidbit #3
Flash Bulletin!

Scott would love to get married and have a family — "I love kids. They're so cute! I'd like two girls and a boy. I like the name Jordan for a boy and Remi for a girl."

Little-Known Fact: Scott needs glasses to read.

Faves

FIVE Song: "'Satisfied' — I'm really into ballads."

Book: *The Hobbit*

Place: Florida

Food: Pizza with cheese, tomato, and ham; simple fast food — "I like plain food, plain ham, plain chicken; I'm a fussy eater."

Drink: Cherry Coke

Snacks: British pastries like Rich Tea fingers and Jammy Dodgers

Midnight Snack: Cheese

Toast Spread: Marmite

Fast Food: Burger King

School Subject: Drama

Clothing Designer: Tommy Hilfiger

Vacation: "A sunbathing holiday"

Holiday: Christmas

Christmas Dinner: "A burger and chips! I hate turkey, veggies, and stuffing!"

Sports: Basketball and skating

Aftershave: CKBe, Addiction by Fabergé

Actress: Alicia Silverstone

Sports Star: Michael Jordan

Way to Relax: "Seeing my pals and family back in Essex"

ABS
The Hunky One

R ichard "Abs" Breen — he's the buff boy of FIVE — even has some pretty macho dreams. Like what? Well, like being a race-car driver. Abs was *beyond* control when he found out that FIVE was going to be filming part of their long-form video, *FIVE Inside,* at England's top race-car training center, Brands Hatch. When the guys walked in the front gate, Abs was already asking, "When do we get to race?"

There *is* another side to Mr. Macho, though. You might be surprised to know that underneath all that bluff and bluster Abs is really a bit of a "mama's boy." An only child whose parents divorced when he was still small, Abs was basically raised by his mum, Kay. His dad, Turan, lived nearby and spent quite a bit of time with Abs, but for the most part, it was Abs and his mum.

Abs told a Scholastic reporter: "I was very well behaved as a child because of my mum. I was polite. And I wasn't given everything. I was made to wait for things. I remember my first keyboard. It was like twenty pounds [$30], and for a single mother, twenty pounds was a lot of money. So I had to wait six months, but when I did get it, it was like I cleaned it every day and kept it nice. I've still got it till this day!"

When Abs hit his teen years, he rebelled a bit, and recalls: "I started becoming a bad boy. I started hanging around with the wrong people. I lied to my mum and said we were hanging at a friend's house when I was really going out to clubs and stuff like that. But I never had fights or anything. I never really got into trouble, because my mum had taught me right from wrong and it's stayed with me all my life."

Still close to his mum, Abs admits he misses her since he's moved out to be part of FIVE. Whenever he has a few days off, he heads right back home and lets Kay pamper him. She cooks his favorite meals and invites all the relatives over to visit. "She's very proud of me now . . . and I'm proud of her!" asserts Abs.

In his own words:
• What FIVE means to Abs •

F is for fun

I is for ingenious

V is for vicious (when we're onstage)

E is for everything (you'll ever need!)

Abs Stats

Full Name: Richard Abidin Breen
Nickname: Abs
B-day: June 29, 1979
Birthplace: Hackney, East London, England
Astro Sign: Cancer
Height: 5'9"
Hair/Eyes: Black/Brown (with a hint of green)
Parents: Turan and Kay (they are divorced)
Siblings: None
School: Italia Conti Performing Arts College
Pets: Two cockatiels named Kiwi and Banana

Tender Tidbits

Childhood Hero: Michael Jackson
Roommate in the FIVE House: Scott
Ideal Girl: Danielle Brent, who stars on the British soap *Hollyoaks* as "Gina Patricks"
Best Friend: Paul Danan, who is also on *Hollyoaks*
Hobbies: DJ-ing, music, going to films, computer games
Major Dislikes: "Smoking, drugs, drinking, and fake people"
Boxers or Briefs: Boxers

Tidbit #4
Headline News!
Abs wants to get a tattoo — but "my mum won't let me."

Abs confesses he has a strange morning ritual: "I usually run around with a blanket wrapped around me. My feet are cold in the morning, so I put my socks on first."

18

Silliest Spending Splurge: A pair of cat's-eye contact lenses

Secret Ambition: To be a race-car driver. Abs got the chance to drive on the Brands Hatch training center track when FIVE filmed their long-form video *FIVE Inside*.

Photo Phobia: "You should see my passport photo — it's terrible. I look like a monster!"

Self-Analysis: "I've just discovered I have big mood swings. I'm also a bit of a romantic."

Worst Fear: "I don't like any kind of flying insect."

Cookin' With Abs: "I'm not too good in the kitchen. I can cook a mean lasagna and some good pasta, but that's about it. I don't make my own sauce or anything, but it still tastes good."

Good-Luck Charm: A Turkish eye amulet

Faves

FIVE Song: "'My Song' — It's jungle music. It's really raw and it's got a strong base and drums."

Food: His mum's shepherd's pie

Drink: Water

Snack: Chocolate

School Subjects: Art and drama

Vacation: Barbados

Holiday: Christmas

Christmas Dinner: "Stuffing — I like stuffing sandwiches. And Yorkshire puddings."

Theme Park: EuroDisney

Video Game: PlayStation's *Heart of Darkness*

Sport: Basketball, rugby — all sports

Aftershave: Tommy, Polo, Jean Paul Gaultier

Musical Artist: Michael Jackson

Sports Shoes: Nike

Cuddle Toy: "Zebby" — a stuffed zebra

Way to Relax: "I like to watch fish."

Childhood Memory: "Going to Australia with my mum when I was twelve."

Abs can't help smiling when he admits he's never had a romantic breakup!

SEAN
The Young One

Sean Kieran Conlon — he's the baby of FIVE, but when you talk to him, you would never think so. As a matter of fact, even J (the oldest one) has said that Sean is the most mature of the group. That's not news to Sean, who told a *Smash Hits* reporter: "I never really feel my age, and I didn't when I was younger, either. When I was four, I felt five, then when I was six, I felt eight. I always felt older somehow."

But sometimes Sean's "maturity" is mistaken for arrogance. Because Sean is a little more laid-back than the other lads, some people have even described him as being a little bit stuck on himself.

He's anything but.

"I've got a lot of respect for myself, but I don't take myself too seriously," Sean explained to *Smash Hits*. "I'm quite straight-faced and my mannerisms are quite serious, too, so people always think I'm dead serious, but I'm not always. I do like to have a laugh."

Sean doesn't have "an attitude" and he's not a phony. He sums up his personality with one word: *genuine*. What you see is what you get. "If I'm in a bad mood, I'm in a bad mood," he says. "I'm not gonna act all smiley. And I'm not gonna lie in interviews to try and come across as something different. What's the point? I'm just myself, right?"

Sean is a typical teen who happens to work in a very adult world. But while he's got a good business mind, there are a few things that can turn Sean into trembling jelly. "I'm scared stiff of horror films," Sean told *Live & Kicking* magazine. "If I watch one, I'm terrified when I go to bed. My imagination runs wild!"

- **Sean's fave 5 things are . . . "**
  1. Writing music
  2. Listening to music
  3. Girls
  4. Being in the band
  5. Sleeping

Sean Stats

Full Name: Sean Kieran Conlon
Nickname: Gungi
B-day: May 20, 1981
Birthplace: Leeds, England
Astro Sign: Taurus
Height: 5'9"
Hair/Eyes: Black/Brown
Parents: Dennis and Kate (they are divorced)
Siblings: Sisters Charlotte and Katrina, and brother, Dominic
Pets: Two dogs

Tender Tidbits

Childhood Hero: Eddie Murphy
Roommate in the FIVE House: None — he had his own bedroom.
Hobby: Writing songs
Major Dislike: "People who think they're the best"
Boxers or Briefs: Boxers
Most Embarrassing Moment: "When I knocked over a table full of food at a party"
Photo Phobia: "I'm not very confident about how I look, so I'm not keen about having my picture taken."
Self-Analysis: "I'm shy and emotional . . . laid-back and chilled."
Alter Ego: "I'd like to be called 'Jermaine.' I think I was going to be called that when I was born."

"I can only talk to people when I know them and feel comfortable with them," confesses Sean.

Takeout Food: Chinese, Indian, fries and curry sauce
Video Games: Nintendo 64 — especially the game *Goldeneye*
School Subject: Music
Holiday: Christmas
Christmas Dinner: "Stuffing and turkey — especially turkey skin, mmmmmm!"
Sport: Rugby
Aftershave: Dune and Polo Sport
Actress: Meg Ryan
Singers: R. Kelly, Marvin Gaye
Musical Group: Jackson Five
Sports Shoes: Nike
Way to Relax: Playing video games

Tidbit #5
Extra! Extra!
Scott is the only member of FIVE who can make Sean blush!

faves

FIVE Song: "'Slam Dunk (Da Funk)' — it's about nothing at all. It's just pop. It's just music."
Place: Sweden
Color: Dark green
Food: Pasta and Spanish omelets
Drink: Coca-Cola
Snacks: Toffee Crisp chocolate bars and cheese-and-onion chips

"Life is what you make it," says Sean. "And I'm just trying to make mine what I want it to be."

J

The Tuff One

Jason Paul Brown is the oldest member of FIVE. Because of that *and* his bodybuilder, pumped-up look, he's gotten a rep as a rough-and-tough boss-lad. True or false? Well, a little bit of both.

J has never tried to assume the "Big Daddy" role in FIVE. He's done the exact opposite. "When I joined FIVE and realized I was the oldest, I made the mental decision *not* to assume the leadership role because it would distance me from the other guys," he told *Smash Hits* very candidly. "If there are decisions to be made, I'll take charge, but I don't control the group."

A one-time active bodybuilder, J explains he started working out because he "had nothing else to do. I wasn't employed, so I used to go to the gym about five or six times a week. But it got a bit stupid. . . . I weighed fifteen stone [210 lbs] back then. I had a fat neck and huge arms."

Though he's slimmed down since then, J is still a pretty solid guy. And J feels that's one reason some people mistakenly have a tough-guy image of him. "I've been wrongly accused of all sorts of stuff," he told *Tops of the Pops* mag. "It *must* be the way I look!"

But as everyone knows, looks can be deceiving. Even if J *could* control a situation physically, he wouldn't. "I detest people who bully," he told *Smash Hits*. "It's a sad and pathetic thing to do. If anything, I got into trouble [in school] for trying to stop people bullying."

So who is the *real* J? "I have a very, very soft, gentle side," admits J to the *Smash Hits* reporter. "I'm not scared or embarrassed to show it. I don't know how to explain it. Romantic? Extremely. I think everyone's got that side."

That's the side J's fans have come to know and love.

In his own words:
• What FIVE means to J •

F is for fantastic
I is for interesting
V is for vocal
E is for experience

"My special teddy bear is the one my sister gave me for my twenty-first birthday."

J Stats

Full Name: Jason Paul Brown

Nickname: J

B-day: June 13, 1976

Birthplace: Aldershot, Warrington, England

Childhood Homes: England, Canada, and Germany (his dad was in the British Armed Services)

Astro Sign: Gemini

Height: 5'10"

Hair/Eyes: Brown/Blue

Parents: Justin and Marilyn

Siblings: Older sister, Donna

Pets: He used to have fish, a hamster, several rottweilers, and cats.

Early Jobs: Worked in a warehouse; sold magazines

Tender Tidbits

Roommate in the FIVE House: Rich

Dream Girl: "I particularly like dark-haired girls . . . not too much makeup."

Hobby: Working out

Major Dislike: Cabs in London

Boxers or Briefs: Calvin Klein boxers

Optimist or Pessimist: "I'm the world's biggest pessimist. If things are going well, I'll think, 'This is going to end soon.' I can't help it."

Photo Phobia: "I'd rather be performing than having my photo taken."

Self-Analysis: "Like a true Gemini I have loads of different sides. I can be the life and soul of the party and the next minute [be] really quiet."

Worst Quality: "I've always had a short temper and when we work such long hours, I get tired, so I get [stressed] with everything."

Best Bud in FIVE: "Sean — he's like a younger brother."

With the money he earns from FIVE, J says he's "gonna buy a recording studio."

Buff Boy: J used to be a bodybuilder — he has a 16" neck to prove it!

Heritage: "I'm mixed race: my dad's biracial and chocolate fudge cake, a carton of juice, some prawns, strawberries, and a CD."

> "I don't really believe in superstitions," insists J, "but I still won't walk under ladders and all that kind of thing. Sad, isn't it?"

half my family is Jamaican. I don't think any of the fans know that and they should." (*Smash Hits*)

Worst Practical Joke: J sprayed stink-bomb powder in the bathroom when FIVE first moved into their house — and locked Abs in there for hours! (*Top of the Pops*)

Body Piercing: He wears a ring under his right eyebrow. "It hangs lower than most people's, because when I first had it done, it almost got pulled out. I can't see it really — it just looks a bit like a big eyelash!" (*Live & Kicking*)

First Music Bought: "A record by Doug E. Fresh and the Get Fresh Crew"

Shopping Basket Peek: "You'd find

faves

FIVE Song: "'I Got the Feelin' — it's just a really good summer track. I prefer upbeat stuff."

Author: Dean Coontz

Movie: *Dawn of the Dead*

Places: Canada and Sweden

Takeout Restaurant: A Chinese place called Wok Away

Food: Chinese (J's *least* fave food is caviar. "Who'd pay all that money for a few salty eggs?!")

Drink: Orange juice

Snack: Sour-cream-and-onion potato chips

School Subjects: English and Physics

Vacation: Crete, an island off the coast of Greece

Country: Sweden

Hangout: A club called East in Sweden

Season: Summer

Holiday: Christmas

Christmas Dessert: "Mince pies with loads of cream"

Video Game: PlayStation

Sport: Football

Aftershave: Versace's Dreamer

Toothpaste: Colgate Total

Actress: Vanessa Williams

Music: Hip-hop and '80s soul

Musical Artist: Tupac Shakur

Sports Shoes: Nike

Puppy love? J always has to have something to hug — especially a pup like this. FIVE loves meeting their fans at autograph signings.

FIVE took over the London Virgin Megastore when they appeared there in February 1998.

Sean, Abs, and J on the set of their video *Now and Forever*.

Looking like a cross between Prodigy and KISS, (l. to r.) J, Sean, Abs, Scott, and Rich posed with their Select UK Award, which is voted on by viewers, at the 1998 MTV Europe Music Awards in Milan, Italy.

STAGE Foto Fun

A perk of being a pop star: You get to do crazy photo shoots.

FIVE is looking forward to doing a major arena world tour!

FIVE became the star attraction at Sam Goody's in Universal City, California. This stop was during their first promo tour of the U.S. in the summer of '98.

FIVE has paid their performing dues in small clubs and promo tour appearances, like this one at a British radio station.

Rich before the *Now and Forever* cameras.

At another radio station appearance, Scott recalls, "J started doing the wrong dance routine for 'The Things You Do,' making us all laugh. But the fans were really cool!"

It's hard work being pop stars!

STAGE Foto Fun

Rich knows how to pose for the camera — but did you know he never goes anywhere without his own camera? Watch out, he may catch you in his lens!

"I'm not your average guy who plays the field," says Scott. "I just want to be a nice sort of bloke!"

FIVE was proud to participate in Nickelodeon's 1998 *The Big Help* benefit show.

FIVE makes a surprise visit to a *Seventeen* magazine party in New York.

FIVE's
True Confessions

Sean's Hair Scare
"I had a big Afro when I was eleven. I was trying to grow it but it went wrong." (*Smash Hits*)

Abs' Confession Session
"I killed my grandad's fish! I was young. It was one of those black goldfish with the big boogley eyes and it was sweet. I filled up the tank with ketchup because I thought he was hungry! My grandad wondered how it happened and I denied it — ahhh, I feel bad now!" (*Smash Hits*)

J, Mr. Cool
"I once told this girl that I had a really nice car to try and impress her, but then she asked me to pick her up in it. So I had to think very quickly and say I'd sold it!" (*Mizz*)

Rich's Mirror, Mirror on the Wall
"I often think that I am a proper loon. I talk to myself. I walk past a mirror and pull a *daft* face [make a silly face] and laugh at myself, then carry on walking." (*Smash Hits*)

ment and record company and said, 'We're not asking you if we can cancel, we're telling you, we're *not* going to Taiwan.' That was it — we'd really had enough!" (*Bliss*)

Sean, Hairstylist

"Scott's hair — it's so perfect, it just drives me mad. So once, I went to fluff it all up, to mess it up, and Scott bit me! He wasn't happy!" (*Mizz*)

Abs' Little White Lie

"The biggest fib I ever told was to my teachers at school when the band was just starting out. I said one of my friends was really ill in the hospital — somehow they found out that I'd been lying, phoned my mum, and she phoned my manager!" (*Mizz*)

Scott's Dear Diary

"I keep a diary, and I wouldn't want anyone reading it. I write everything from work stuff, like things I've been doing in the day, to all my personal feelings. I always carry it in my bag with me so no one will ever get the chance to see it!" (*TV Hits*)

Scott's Rebellion

"Early August 1998 was my lowest point. We went from promoting in America, to Australia, then straight back to London to film the video for 'Everybody Get Up.' We had one day off to sleep, then we left for Australia for a week, then on to Japan for another week, working all the time. After that we were supposed to go to Taiwan, but we really couldn't face it. We actually turned round to our manage-

J — Boy Power

"My sister gave me a facial once. I had cleansers and tonics and all sorts of stuff massaged on to my face — it was lovely! It shouldn't just be women who are pampered, you know." (*Live & Kicking*)

Abs, Mr. Manners
"I went to this posh restaurant recently and there were all these knives and forks. I ended up copying everyone else." (*Live & Kicking*)

Abs' Fave Childhood Toy
"My bikes have always been my favorites — I started off with a little police bike with a light on it. I used to pretend I was a bus driver for some strange reason." (*Live & Kicking*)

Sean, Nature Boy
"My favorite smell is grass being cut. It's nice — unless you've got hay fever, which I do. . . . It reminds me of summertime and being a kid." (*TV Hits*)

Scott's Lucky Charm
"I have to say that my mum and dad are my lucky charms. Oh, and my bracelet — I never take it off." (*Live & Kicking*)

What Makes Rich Cry
"I can't bear to see other people upset. If someone's really sad, even if I don't know them that well, it makes me get really upset."

Then you'd go down and it would be deadly quiet." (*Live & Kicking*)

Abs' Fish Tale

"If I could make one thing illegal, it would be anchovies. Flippin' hate 'em, man. They're so disgusting, I'm always picking 'em off stuff. They make me gag. Fish are cool — it's just anchovies I don't like." (*Smash Hits*)

Scott's Dream Mate on a Desert Island

"A while ago, I would've said Alicia Silverstone, but I think I've grown up quite a bit since I've been in the band. Obviously I'm still an outgoing, nutty sort of person, but my views on females are changing. The type of girl I like now doesn't have to have blonde hair and blue eyes — she could have any type of look." (*TV Hits*)

Rich, Lover Boy

"Girls are my weakness! When I meet someone I like, I fall in headfirst — I just think about her nonstop." (*Live & Kicking*)

J's Ghost Story

"I know you'll think it's far-fetched, but my grandparents lived in an old house with a plaque on the wall saying an old highwayman rested here. Sometimes when my sister and I were upstairs, we could hear loads of noises like there was a massive party going on downstairs!

J, the Bratty Little Brother

"I've got an older sister and we used to have bunk beds and she slept on the bottom. Sometimes I'd hide under her bed, wait until she got in it, and then stick my arm up under the mattress and scare her stupid!" (*Live & Kicking*)

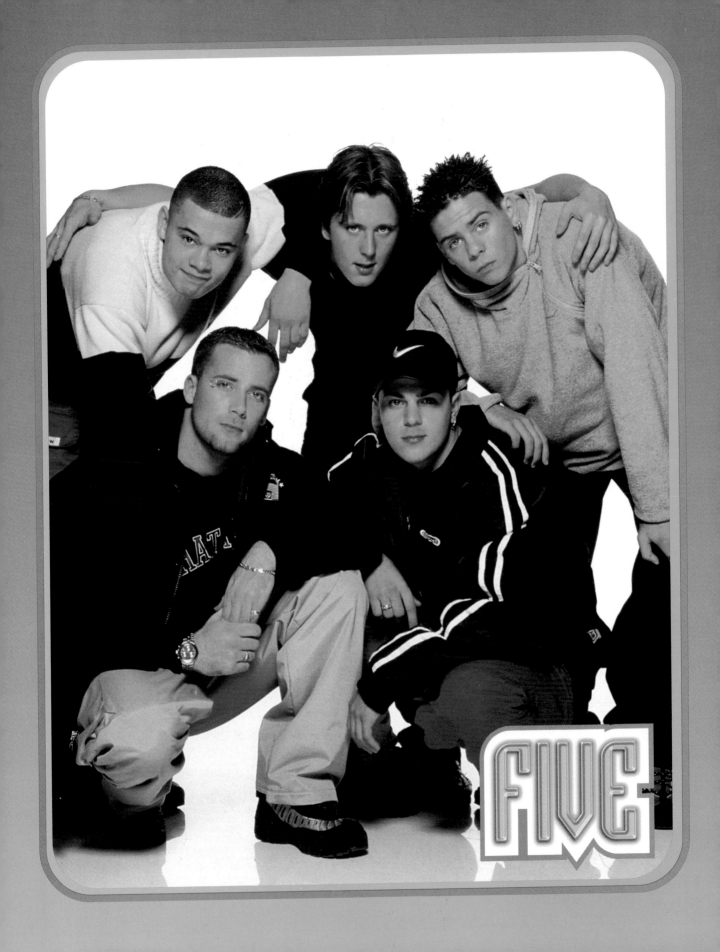

J — Housemates

"Me, Sean, and Rich still live together. . . . Abs and Scott couldn't hack it anymore!" (*Dolly*)

Tattletales!

FIVE Spills the Beans on Each Other!

Rich: "Scott can have bad table manners, like when we go out somewhere nice. To start with, he won't eat anything — all he ever has is a burger and chips with loads of ketchup. And Abs gets in moods where he takes a glass of water, sticks ketchup in it, then salt and pepper, then empties the ashtray into it, sticks in a flower, and mixes it all around." (*Smash Hits*)

J: "Scott's like a kid — he'll only eat fast food or things like mashed potatoes and stuff, so he's always tired. He has no energy and he's always making these [silly] noises. Rich is the more emotional one of the band; you can tell straight away what he's thinking by looking at his face. He's a hippie as well."

Abs: "J is the 'daddy.' He makes sure we're up in the morning and we're where we should be. But he's not the boss, oh, no!"

J: "Sean's lazy! I do his wash and his ironing for him!"

Rich: "Sean is definitely not soppy although he has his soft side, too. He has strong opinions and there's no changing his mind."

Sean: "Abs is laid-back but strong-headed. Sometimes he's completely silent; other times he won't stop talking."

Scott: "Rich is very emotional. He's the model of the band and can also be quite shy until he gets to know you."

Group Gab:

• **Who's the biggest joker?**
All: "Scott!"
J: "Scott is just out of control — he is the biggest kidder in the group."

• **Who likes to party the most?**
J: "Me and Sean."
Sean: "The others go to bed."

• **Who's the most romantic?**
Rich: "Abs!"
Abs: "No! I'm not — we all are."

• **Who gets away with the most?**
Rich: "Sean gets away with everything."

J: "Sean gets away with doing absolutely nothing all the time."

Rich: "In over a year, not once has he ironed any clothes or washed one single thing."

Love Notes
Rich, Scott,
Check Out FIVE's

From Sean, Abs, & J
Smooth Moves

RICH

♥ "There is a certain feeling that singles a girl out from the others. As soon as you see her you think, 'She's the one!' She really stands out in a crowd. If it's love, your heart skips a beat, you get butterflies in your stomach, you find it difficult to eat sometimes." (Internet interview)

♥ "Love is intense, hard, and it hurts big-time, but it's worth it." (*Live & Kicking*)

♥ "I'd like to be with someone for a couple of years before getting married. I don't believe in this getting married after three months stuff." (*TV Hits*)

♥ "Worst breakup? . . . I'd just turned seventeen and had been going out with this girl for about a year. She was my first love. Then she went away to Greece and met someone else. She broke my heart big-time." (*Jump*)

♥ "I'm a good boyfriend because if I promise I'll do something, I *will* do it, no matter what happens. I think that's why people tend to trust and depend on me 'cause they know I won't break a promise." (*Smash Hits*)

♥ "To get over a broken heart, I think you need a bit of time alone to cry. You get it all out of your system. You might sit there thinking, *I need her,* but you can survive." (*Teen*)

SCOTT

♥ "Too much complaining — that usually means the relationship isn't working out, and it's time to just end it." (*Jump*)

♥ "I've been in love. I know what it's like. Your heart skips a beat and you act all funny. You can't stop thinking about the girl, you phone [her] up even when you've got absolutely nothing to say. I'm a very jealous person [when I'm] in love, to tell you the truth." (*Smash Hits*)

♥ "When my girlfriend finished with me, I lost it. I couldn't handle it. In fact, I burst blood vessels in my eyes because I cried so much. We were in Sweden and I was crying so much I couldn't see. Rich came up to try and comfort me. It wasn't a good day." (*Big!*)

♥ "I've never said 'I love you' and not meant it." (*Big!*)

SEAN

♥ "I've always wanted to have a girl who likes me for me, and I think the only way I can do that — because I don't trust many people now — is to go out with someone I knew before we got famous." (*Smash Hits*)

♥ "I look for someone who acts very feminine, although I don't like a lot of nail polish or makeup." (*Live & Kicking*)

♥ "I went out with this girl when I was about nine. She was the first girl I ever kissed. Five years later we started dating again." (*Jump*)

ABS

♥ "Love is being able to tell that person absolutely anything and wanting to be with her every second." (*Live & Kicking*)

♥ "You know you're in love when there's a real connection between you: You have your own little in-jokes; you can always catch [her] glance across a crowded room; you can always tell what's running through [her] mind." (*Smash Hits*)

J

♥ "The first thing I notice about a girl is her mouth — I like nice lips." (*Live & Kicking*)

♥ "Love can sometimes be cruel, sometimes be kind."

♥ "People perceive me to be the kind of bloke who [doesn't have serious] romances. Not so. I've had only long relationships, and I don't mess about." (*Smash Hits*)

♥ "My confidence [sometimes] drops really low. I've got two different moods — loud and quiet. When I'm really quiet, I just can't approach [girls]. Even if I'm told some girl fancies me, I can't make the first move." (*Live & Kicking*)

Discography

5IVE
(CD — UK Version)
Released 1997 - Debuted at #1
- "Slam Dunk (Da Funk)"
- "When the Lights Go Out"
- "Everybody Get Up"
- "Got the Feelin'"
- "It's the Thing You Do"
- "Human"
- "Until the Time Is Through"
- "Satisfied"
- "Partyline 555-On-Line"
- "That's What You Told Me"
- "It's All Over"
- "Don't You Want It"
- "Shake"
- "Cold Sweat"
- "Straight Up Funk"
- "My Song"

5IVE
(CD — European Version)
Released 1997
- "It's the Thing You Do" (European version)
- "Straight Up Funk"

- "Human"
- "Shake"
- "Cold Sweat"
- "Don't You Want It"
- "Switch"

5IVE
(CD — Australian Version)
Released 1997
- "Slam Dunk (Da Funk)"
- "When the Lights Go Out"
- "Everybody Get Up"
- "Got the Feelin'"
- "It's the Thing You Do"
- "Human" (the FIVE remix)
- "Until the Time Is Through"
- "Satisfied"
- "Partyline 555-On-Line"
- "That's What You Told Me"
- "It's All Over"
- "Don't You Want It"
- "Shake"
- "Cold Sweat"
- "Straight Up Funk"
- "My Song"
- "Track 55" aka "Switch"

5IVE
(CD — U.S. Version)
Released July 15, 1998
- "When the Lights Go Out"
- "That's What You Told Me"
- "It's the Thing You Do"
- "When I Remember When"
- "Slam Dunk (Da Funk)"
- "Satisfied"
- "It's All Over"
- "Partyline 555-On-Line"
- "Until the Time Is Through"
- "Everybody Get Up"
- "My Song"
- "Got the Feelin'"

Videos

Slam Dunk (Da Funk)
When the Lights Go Out
Got the Feelin'
Everybody Get Up
FIVE Inside
(long-form video)
Now and Forever
(long-form video)

You've Got Mail!

Go Postal! Go Cyber!...With FIVE!

Official UK/Ireland
FIVE Fan Club:

Costs 18 pounds to join (approximately 30 U.S. dollars)

You receive:
- A numbered **FIVE** gold membership card
- A black backpack with the **FIVE** logo
- 5 color photo cards of Rich, Scott, Abs, Sean, & J
- A full-color poster of FIVE
- A **FIVE** sticker
- A regular newsletter update

Phone: (country & city code) 0891 500055—ask your parents first!

Internet Hook-ups
Arista Records: www.arista.com
(go to the FIVE homepage)

Ultimate Band List: www.ubl.com
(go to FIVE links — there are over 100!)

The future of FIVE

"We're just five young boys having a laugh," J told MTV, "and we're going to appreciate it until the day it comes to an end, like everybody should. You should never sit there and be complacent and think, 'Yeah, I deserve this.'"

FIVE *does* deserve all the awards and attention they've gotten — because they've paid their dues. They've racked up thousands of frequent-flyer miles by making appearances all over the world, from right in their London backyard to Australia, Japan, and the U.S.A. Performing in front of audiences from five to 5,000, and eventually 50,000, Rich, Scott, Abs, Sean, and J have pushed themselves to the limit — existing on no sleep, fast food, and no time off. But they feel it's all worth it.

Their future plans include everything and anything possible: more top-of-the-charts CDs, more awards, more concerts, more appearances, more autographs, and perhaps even their own recording studio and label, an international TV series, and feature films. It's all there for the taking . . . and FIVE is ready! Are you?